# WHEN DINOS DAWNED, MAMMALS GOT MUNCHED, & PTEROSAURS TOOK FLIGHT

## A Cartoon Prehistory of Life in the Triassic

WRITTEN AND ILLUSTRATED BY

## Hannah Bonner

NATIONAL GEOGRAPHIC

WASHINGTON, D.C.

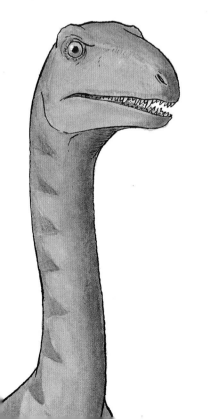

**To my aunt, Rebecca Rieger, for all her support of my artistic endeavors**

## ACKNOWLEDGMENTS

A number of scientists kindly agreed to contribute their time and knowledge to this project. The wonderful paleobotanist Evelyn Kustatscher of the Museum of Nature South Tyrol in Italy was my principal plants advisor. University of California Berkeley paleoecologists Cindy Looy and Ivo Duijnstee helped me recreate *Pleuromeia* for the opening scene. Heidi Holmes and John Anderson were both extremely generous in helping me reconstruct the plants and insects of the Molteno formation of South Africa (pages 28—29). Geologist David Kidder at Ohio University in Athens helped with climate and extinctions. Piero Gianolla of the University of Ferrara in Italy gave me a hand with all things Tethys. Finally, Corwin Sullivan, now at the Institute of Vertebrate Paleontology and Paleoanthropology in Beijing, China, was at my virtual side the entire time, contributing to everything from the big picture of how Triassic vertebrates evolved to the exact position of the bony plates on the back of *Ticinosuchus*. If Corwin had his way, every tiniest detail of every vertebrate illustrated would be perfect. It has never been truer that where this is not the case, the mistakes are mine alone.

Many thanks as well to all the scientists who provided me with papers, contacts, and answers to my many questions: Kenneth Angielczyk, Analía Artabe, Kay Behrensmeyer, Matt Celeskey, Marlene Hill Donnelly, Flavia Gargiulo, Hans Hagdorn, Conrad Labandeira, John Maisey, Carl Mehling, Mary Parrish, and Luis Pomar. If I have forgotten someone, please know that I am grateful for your help. I also want to thank the participants in an excellent geology workshop and field trip to the Southern Alps in September 2010 for patiently explaining many aspects of Triassic geology to me.

Of course, none of this would ever have coalesced into a book without the terrific team at National Geographic Children's Books. I have felt like a singer who is lucky enough to be accompanied by the best musicians: editor Jennifer Emmett on lead guitar, designer David Seager on keyboards, designer Ruthie Thompson on bass and drums (that's right, she can play two instruments at once!), and Jean Mendoza plus the rest of the staff on backup vocals. Thanks also to Nancy Laties Feresten, the ongoing godmother of this series, whose idea it was to do books about life before the dinosaurs.

And last but not least, a big thanks from the bottom of my heart to my family and friends for their love, support, and excellent feedback at various stages of the book.

Book design by Hannah Bonner and Ruthie Thompson with David M. Seager, Art Director. The text is set in Gilgamesh medium.

Library of Congress Cataloging-in-Publication Data
Bonner, Hannah.
  When dinos dawned, mammals got munched, and Pterosaurs took flight: a cartoon prehistory of life in the Triassic / Hannah Bonner.
      p. cm.
  Includes bibliographical references and index.
    ISBN 978-1-4263-0862-8 (hardback)
    ISBN 978-1-4263-0863-5 (lib. bdg.)
  1. Paleontology—Triassic—Comic books, strips, etc.—Juvenile literature.
  2. Graphic novels.  I. Title.
  QE732.B66 2012
  567.9—dc23
                          2011029212
Printed in China

11/RRDS/1

# TABLE of CONTENTS

# WELCOME TO THE TRIASSIC

It's 7 a.m. in South Africa, at the very beginning of the Triassic period. The day has barely begun, and it's already unbearably hot out. Dozens of *Lystrosaurus*, low-slung animals that look like small pigs, are busy scrunching their way through a stand of corn-size plants called *Pleuromeia*.

MORE SCORCHING WEATHER AHEAD, FOLKS. WE RECOMMEND STAYING IN YOUR BURROWS IN THE MIDDLE OF THE DAY.

110°
120°
95°

Wherever we go in the early days of the Triassic we find the same thing: a hot, dry landscape, smallish plants, and lots of *Lystrosaurus* eating them. The planet is struggling to recover from the biggest extinction of all time, and while there is a fair amount of life, there is very little variety and a conspicuous absence of anything big. There are no big animals, and trees and forests are nowhere to be seen.

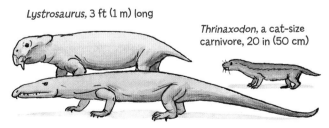

*Lystrosaurus*, 3 ft (1 m) long

*Thrinaxodon*, a cat-size carnivore, 20 in (50 cm)

The biggest carnivore, *Proterosuchus*, was only about 5 ft (1.5 m) long.

# SURVIVING THE BIG ONE

Let's travel back in time a half million years to the end of the Permian period. We're in Siberia. Enormous lava flows are creeping over the landscape, scorching everything in their path. Where the lava reaches a lake or a marsh, it boils the water instantly, sending up huge columns of steam. These are the Siberian Traps, where volcanic activity spewed molten rock over an area twice the size of Alaska. Many scientists think the Siberian Traps were one of the main causes of the giant extinction.

With the lava came huge amounts of carbon dioxide ($CO_2$) and other greenhouse gases. The planet was already hot and dry, and the extra $CO_2$ turned it into an oven. The oceans became stagnant, with very little oxygen ($O_2$), which killed most of the sea life.

Only about 10 percent of plant and animal species made it through to the Triassic. Every life-form alive today descends from this handful of tough survivors.

# THE RETURN OF THE FORESTS

**W**e're now in France, eight million years after the extinction. The Siberian Traps have finally stopped belching gases, and life is getting back on its feet. Forests are just beginning to make a comeback. The conifers (the group that includes pines and firs) are doing especially well, and bugs both old and new are crawling among the leaves and buzzing through the warm air.

Mayflies

**NEW!**

*Grauvogelia,*
the oldest known fly

*Triadotypus* was a huge dragonfly, with a 1 ft (30 cm) wingspan. The other insects shown were the same size or smaller than their modern relatives.

**NEW!**

Tiny *Rosamygale* is the earliest known ancestor of tarantulas 1/10 in (2.5 mm).

Lots of cockroaches and many kinds of beetles

Assorted leaf-hopper and grasshopper ancestors

The trees are *Voltzia,* a conifer that survived the end-Permian extinction.

*Aethophyllum,* a small, grassy conifer

*Pelourdea,* a conifer with long, flat leaves

**WORLD'S OLDEST SPECIES!**

*Eocyclotosaurus,* a big amphibian, 6 ft (3 m)

Three-eyed *Triops cancriformis* is still alive in Europe today.

*Dipteronotus,* 2 in (5 cm)

*Triops cancriformis,* 3 in (8 cm)

*Clytiopsis,* a crayfish, 1.5 in (4 cm)

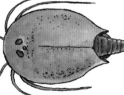

## The Arms Race Is Back

Predators just got bigger, and so did the plant-eaters. In China, for instance, relatives of *Lystrosaurus* such as *Sinokannemeyeria* (an awfully long name—why don't we dub it Potato-face instead?) were the size of a small cow. Stalking two Potato-faces is *Shansisuchus*, a ten-foot-long (3 meters) early relative of dinosaurs and crocodiles.

# THE TRIASSIC PLANET

The Triassic is the first period of the famous Mesozoic era. Partway through the Triassic, the sea flooded Europe for about ten million years, leaving behind a layer of rock full of fossil seashells sandwiched between two layers of nonmarine rock. A 19th-century German geologist named the Triassic for these three layers. You might have already guessed that the name had something to do with the number three (think of words like *triangle*, *tricycle*, or *Triops*, the three-eyed crustacean we saw on page 12).

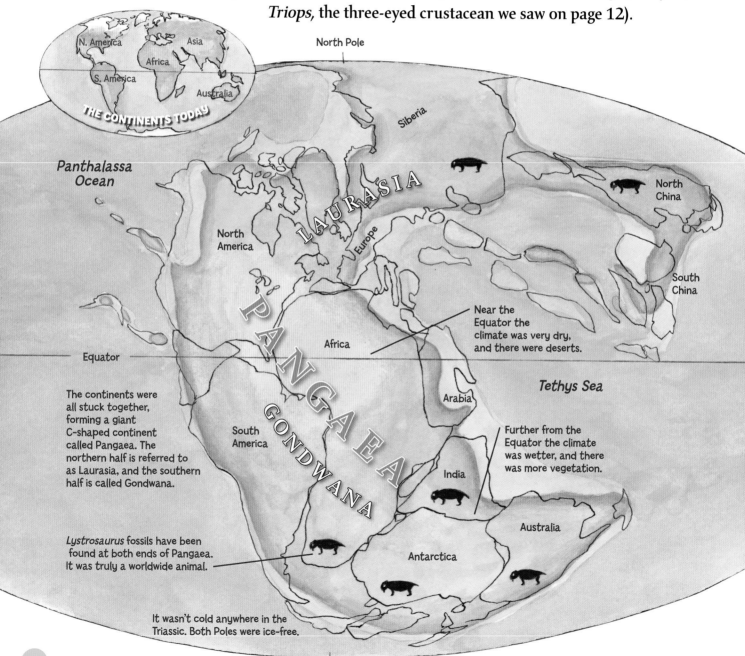

THE CONTINENTS TODAY

N. America · Asia · Africa · S. America · Australia

North Pole

Panthalassa Ocean

Siberia

LAURASIA

North America

Europe

North China

PANGAEA

South China

Near the Equator the climate was very dry, and there were deserts.

Africa

Equator

Tethys Sea

The continents were all stuck together, forming a giant C-shaped continent called Pangaea. The northern half is referred to as Laurasia, and the southern half is called Gondwana.

South America

GONDWANA

Arabia

Further from the Equator the climate was wetter, and there was more vegetation.

India

Australia

*Lystrosaurus* fossils have been found at both ends of Pangaea. It was truly a worldwide animal.

Antarctica

It wasn't cold anywhere in the Triassic. Both Poles were ice-free.

South Pole

We humans probably wouldn't enjoy a trip to the early Triassic. The air was hot and oxygen levels were lower than what we're used to, so besides sweating like pigs we might feel a little weak or dizzy. As plants and ocean life recovered, oxygen levels went up, making it a far more appealing destination.

The climate also got wetter over time, with an especially wet period about halfway through the period. Scientists think that for much of the Triassic, intense wet seasons (monsoons) alternated with very dry seasons, and huge storms were common.

Forests grew almost all the way to the Poles, which were too warm to have any year-round ice. Fossil tree trunks from Antarctica have growth rings that show that even though it wasn't cold out, the trees stopped growing in the winter because of the long months of winter darkness.

*Panthalassa Ocean*

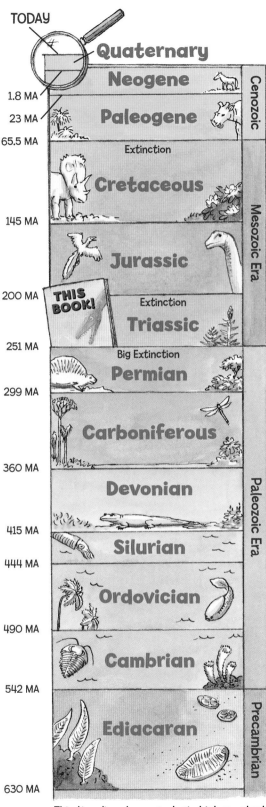

This time line shows geologic history, starting when the seas began to fill with animal life. MA stands for million years ago. (In Latin, "million years" is "mega annum.")

# THE TRIASSIC EXPLOSION

Eudimorphodon

Plateosaurus

Pisanosaurus

Lotosaurus

Coelophysis

Postosuchus

Desmatosuchus

Hyperodapedon

Effigia

Hesperosuchus

Pseudopalatus

Kannemeyeria

Morganucodon, an early mammal

Thrinaxodon

**O**nce ecosystems recovered, life went nuts. So many new plants and animals evolved that some scientists refer to this burst of creativity as the Triassic Explosion. Let's take a look at how the explosion played out among the tetrapods.

Bursting forth from the yellow cloud are the archosaurs and their relatives. From just a few Permian survivors they evolved into a spectacular array of animals including dinosaurs, pterosaurs, and crocodiles. Find out more on pages 22–27 and 37.

Ambling forth from the reddish cloud are our ancestors, the therapsids. They included stocky plant-eaters as well as a line of carnivores that gave rise to the first tiny mammals. More on pages 22–23 and 34–35.

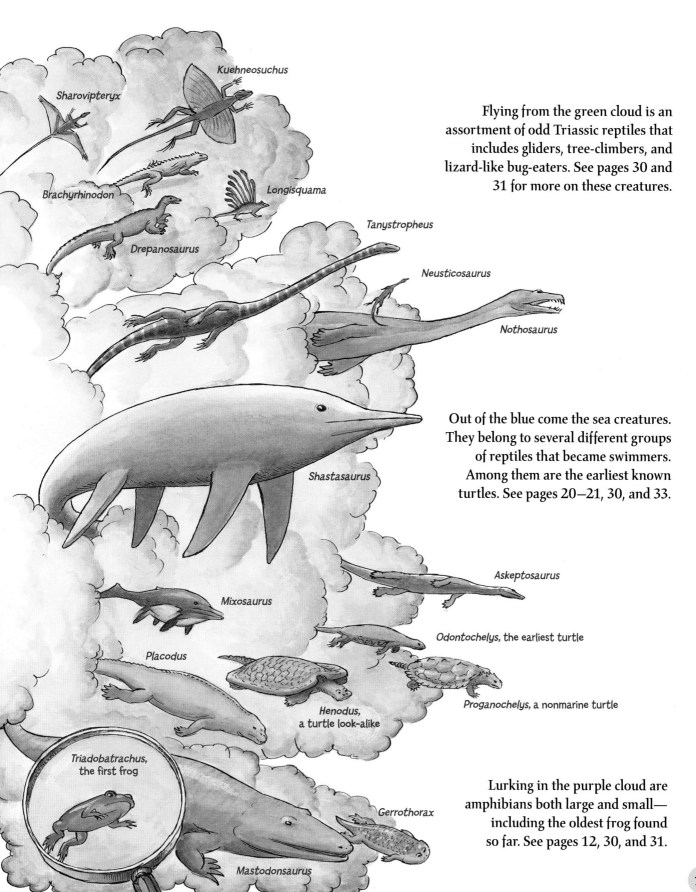

Sharovipteryx

Kuehneosuchus

Brachyrhinodon

Longisquama

Drepanosaurus

Tanystropheus

Neusticosaurus

Nothosaurus

Flying from the green cloud is an assortment of odd Triassic reptiles that includes gliders, tree-climbers, and lizard-like bug-eaters. See pages 30 and 31 for more on these creatures.

Shastasaurus

Out of the blue come the sea creatures. They belong to several different groups of reptiles that became swimmers. Among them are the earliest known turtles. See pages 20–21, 30, and 33.

Askeptosaurus

Mixosaurus

Odontochelys, the earliest turtle

Placodus

Henodus, a turtle look-alike

Proganochelys, a nonmarine turtle

Triadobatrachus, the first frog

Gerrothorax

Lurking in the purple cloud are amphibians both large and small— including the oldest frog found so far. See pages 12, 30, and 31.

Mastodonsaurus

# SUN AND FUN ON THE TETHYS

Of course, the Triassic Explosion didn't happen all at once. It happened gradually, and different plants and animals evolved at different times and in different places.

Let's land on one particular spot on Earth, about a third of the way into the Triassic, and check it out. The Southern Alps, for instance. Uh-oh, where are the mountains? The GPS says they should be right here . . . oh, wait, they haven't been pushed up yet. Instead, we're on the shore of the Tethys Sea, gazing at clear tropical waters dotted with islands and reefs. All the ingredients of a summer paradise are here: lush green vegetation, long sand beaches, seashells . . . and a leopard-size reptile called *Ticinosuchus* scavenging the stinky carcass of a marine reptile called *Cymbospondylus*. Hmm, I guess the Tethys Tourism Bureau still has some kinks to iron out!

*Bjuvia* looks like a banana tree but is really a type of seed plant called a cycad.

Conifers

*Ptilozamites* belongs to an extinct group of seed plants.

*Lepocyclotes*, a spore plant, is related to *Pleuromeia*.

*Protrachyceras*, an ammonite, is a shelled relative of squid, up to 1 ft (30 cm) across.

## TETHYS TRAVEL

# COME SKI IN THE ALPS!

We have the FASTEST nothosaurs at unbeatable prices!

# BEACHCOMBERS' HEAVEN

# SNORKEL IN THE REEFS!

After a 12-million-year gap, reefs are back! Come see sponges, shellfish, algae, cement-like minerals, and a few corals (for true coral reefs, please come back later in the Triassic).

⭐ STARFISH TOURS ⭐

## TETHYS TRAVEL

# BEACHES ARE BACK!

Now that reefs have returned, we have lovely sand made up of bits and pieces of the reef-builders. Come and enjoy!

*Ticinosuchus,*
10 ft (3 m)

*Cymbospondylus,*
up to 30 ft (10 m)

# MARINE MADNESS

**U**nderwater, a revolution was taking place that affected the entire food chain, from plankton all the way to top predators. The oceans offered up a fantastic seafood buffet, and a host of new marine reptiles were ready to eat it.

Placodonts specialized in eating shellfish. *Placodus* had buck teeth in front for grabbing clams and big flat teeth further back for crushing them. 6.5 ft (2 m)

*Nothosaurus,* 10 ft (3 m)

Related to the *placodonts* were the *nothosaurs*. They ranged from large, like *Nothosaurus*, to tiny, like *Neusticosaurus*. 10 in (25 cm)

Clams and other bivalves became very common. Some avoided getting eaten by burrowing into the mud or sand.

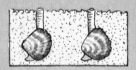

The first oysters

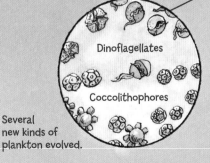

Dinoflagellates

Coccolithophores

Several new kinds of plankton evolved.

The first lobsters

Cephalopods (squid and ammonites) were very common.

SEAWATER DIP

Fish were coming up with many new models, including the earliest flying fish.

20

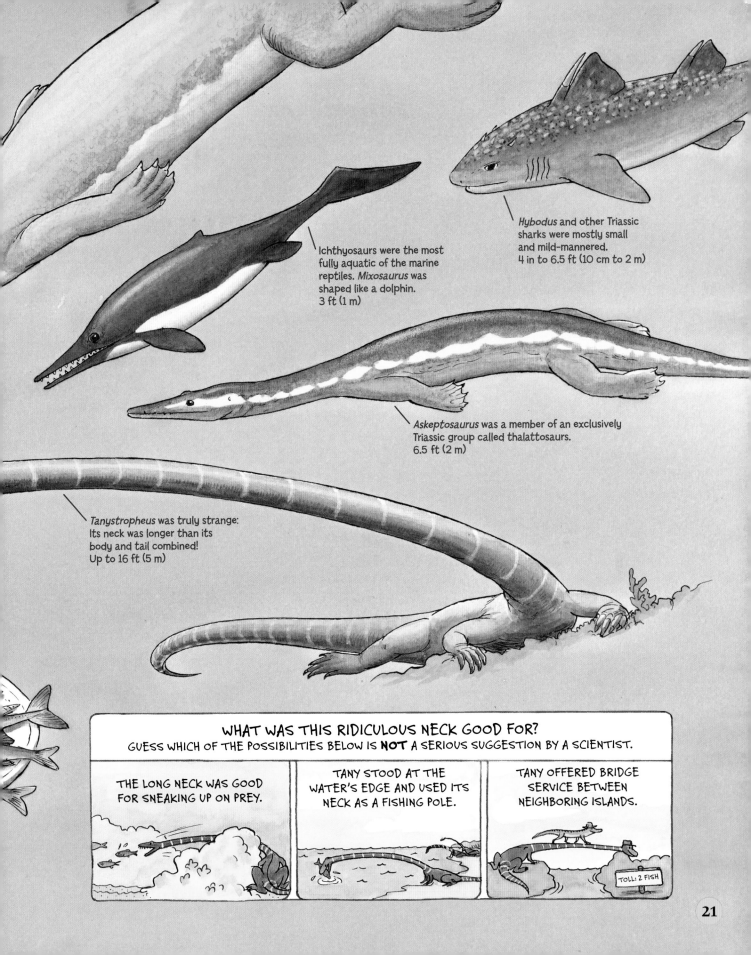

Ichthyosaurs were the most fully aquatic of the marine reptiles. *Mixosaurus* was shaped like a dolphin.
3 ft (1 m)

*Hybodus* and other Triassic sharks were mostly small and mild-mannered.
4 in to 6.5 ft (10 cm to 2 m)

*Askeptosaurus* was a member of an exclusively Triassic group called thalattosaurs.
6.5 ft (2 m)

*Tanystropheus* was truly strange: Its neck was longer than its body and tail combined!
Up to 16 ft (5 m)

## WHAT WAS THIS RIDICULOUS NECK GOOD FOR?
GUESS WHICH OF THE POSSIBILITIES BELOW IS **NOT** A SERIOUS SUGGESTION BY A SCIENTIST.

THE LONG NECK WAS GOOD FOR SNEAKING UP ON PREY.

TANY STOOD AT THE WATER'S EDGE AND USED ITS NECK AS A FISHING POLE.

TANY OFFERED BRIDGE SERVICE BETWEEN NEIGHBORING ISLANDS.

TOLL: 2 FISH

# LORDS OF THE LAND

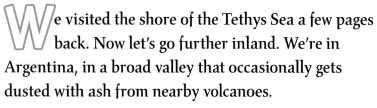

**W**e visited the shore of the Tethys Sea a few pages back. Now let's go further inland. We're in Argentina, in a broad valley that occasionally gets dusted with ash from nearby volcanoes.

The *Dinodontosaurus* below look familiar, don't they? They are related to *Lystrosaurus* and to our friends the Potato-faces. These creatures are therapsids. So is *Massetognathus,* seen scratching itself on the left (fleas hadn't evolved yet, but biting midges had!). You and I are therapsids as well: If you look at the chart on the right, you will see that we come from the same branch of the family tree.

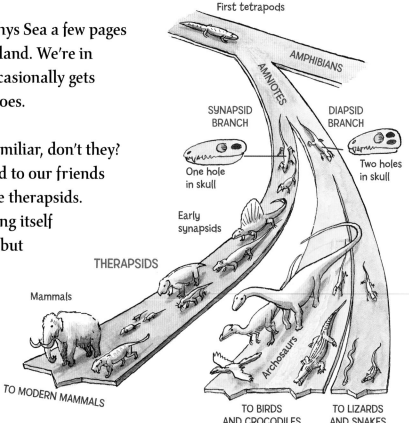

First tetrapods

AMPHIBIANS

AMNIOTES

SYNAPSID BRANCH

One hole in skull

DIAPSID BRANCH

Two holes in skull

Early synapsids

THERAPSIDS

Mammals

Archosaurs

TO MODERN MAMMALS

TO BIRDS AND CROCODILES

TO LIZARDS AND SNAKES

*Massetognathus,*
3 ft (1 m)

*Marasuchus,*
1.7 ft (50 cm)

The therapsids and their ancestors were the world's most successful land animals in the Permian and in the early Triassic, but now their reign was coming to an end: Archosaurs (the group of reptiles that includes dinosaurs, crocodiles, and birds) were on the rise, poised to steal the crown from the therapsids.

SOME LYCOPOD, YOUR HOMELINESS?

**KING THERAPSID'S COURT**

We see two archosaur upstarts in the scene below. One is the tiny *Marasuchus*, an early cousin of dinosaurs (bottom of page 22). The other is *Luperosuchus*, a crocodile relative and top predator who is clearly looking forward to taking over the world one plump therapsid at a time (bottom of this page).

LEAVE ME ALONE! IT'S **MY** CROWN!

C'MON! YOU'VE RULED FOR 160 MILLION YEARS—NOW IT'S MY TURN TO RULE FOR 160 MILLION YEARS.*

*Sure enough, 160 million years later the dinosaurs bit the dust, and mammals, the descendants of therapsids, took over the planet once again. Will we be returning the crown to the descendants of birds and crocodiles 95 million years from now? It would only be fair!

Dinodontosaurus, up to 8 ft (2.4 m)

Luperosuchus, 11 ft (3.5 m)

# THE ARCHOSAURS TAKE OVER

**W**hat a difference 20 million years can make! We're now in Arizona, and the place is swarming with archosaurs. The therapsids haven't disappeared entirely, but they're a lot less common than before.

Early in the Triassic, the archosaurs had split into two branches, the dinosaur branch and the crocodile branch. The crocodile branch got off to a quicker start than the dinosaur branch, and for millions of years croc relatives were more common and much more varied than their dino-branch cousins.

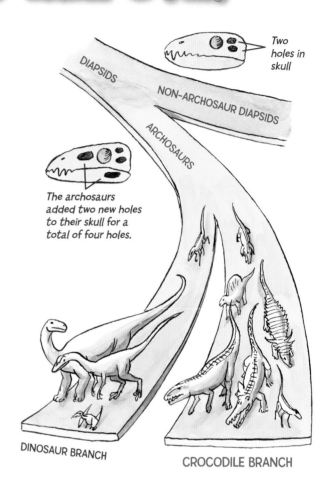

DIAPSIDS

NON-ARCHOSAUR DIAPSIDS

ARCHOSAURS

Two holes in skull

The archosaurs added two new holes to their skull for a total of four holes.

DINOSAUR BRANCH

CROCODILE BRANCH

Postosuchus, 13 ft (4 m)

Hesperosuchus, 4 ft (1.2 m)

# The Ruling Crocs

The crocodile branch produced a crazy number of different creatures, including many dinosaur look-alikes. We saw a few of them, such as *Postosuchus, Effigia,* and *Lotosaurus,* back on the Triassic Explosion page. Bet you thought they were dinos, eh?

THE COURT OF THE CROC KING

*Postosuchus* and other similar meat-eaters were the top predators in their environments. They had tyrannosaur-like heads, but unlike tyrannosaurs they had front legs that could still be used for walking, at least part-time.

Phytosaurs like *Pseudopalatus* were crocodile look-alikes, but were not the direct ancestors of modern crocodiles. Oddly enough, the true ancestors of crocodiles were slender, land-dwelling creatures such as *Hesperosuchus.*

The strangest of the bunch were the aetosaurs: Think reptile with a hint of armadillo and a whiff of pig. Aetosaurs were well armored, and they ate plants and possibly grubs and anything else they could root out with their little, shovel-shaped snouts.

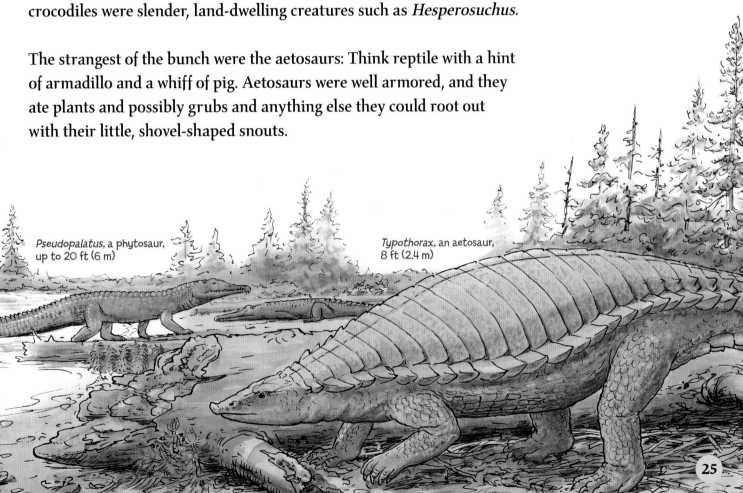

*Pseudopalatus,* a phytosaur, up to 20 ft (6 m)

*Typothorax,* an aetosaur, 8 ft (2.4 m)

# DINOSAURS DAWN

Dinosaurs at last! It's about halfway through the Triassic, and we've landed back in Argentina to find that a medium-size dino predator, *Herrerasaurus*, is busy ripping apart an unfortunate little fellow dinosaur called *Panphagia*.

Fossils of early dinosaurs are quite rare. When dinosaurs first appeared, other archosaurs were still a lot more common. So were an odd bunch of archosaur cousins called rhynchosaurs. Here we see one, *Hyperodapedon,* slinking off in the hopes of not being noticed by *Herrerasaurus*.

The dinosaurs quickly split into three groups. *Herrerasaurus* belongs to the theropod line, which went on to produce *T. rex* and other monster meat-eaters. And who do you think the gigantic long-necks such as *Brachiosaurus* descended from? Believe it or not, from puny creatures like the unfortunate *Panphagia.* Small though *Panphagia* was, scientists can tell from its teeth and bones that it was indeed a very early member of the sauropod line.

EARLY ARCHOSAURS

CROCODILE BRANCH

DINOSAUR BRANCH

Original hip shape

Saurischians keep original shape.

New hip shape in Ornithischians

Ornithischians

Saurischians

TO STEGOSAURS, DUCKBILLS

Sauropods

TO THE LONG-NECKS

Theropods

TO TYRANNOSAURS, BIRDS

Pterosaurs

Exaeretodon
6.5 ft (2 m)

Hyperodapedon,
5 ft (1.5 m)

One of the earliest known ornithischian dinosaurs, *Pisanosaurus*, is also from Argentina. It too was small and unassuming compared to later ornithischians such as stegosaurs and duckbills. All ornithischians, including *Pisanosaurus*, were vegetarians.

*Pisanosaurus*,
3 ft (1 m)

Another Triassic first were the pterosaurs. The pterosaurs were the first tetrapods to truly fly. These distant relatives of dinosaurs appeared on the shores of the Tethys in the late Triassic, but they didn't become common until later, in the Jurassic.

ZZZ

MAN, THAT CROWN WOULD LOOK **SO** GOOD ON ME!

**A DINOSAUR IN THE CROC KING'S COURT**

*Eudimorphodon*,
wingspan,
3.2 ft (1 m)

*Herrerasaurus*,
14.5 ft (4.5 m)

*Panphagia*,
about
5 ft (1.5 m)

27

# MUNCH, MUNCH, MUNCH, PLANTS FOR LUNCH

What were all these new creatures eating? Let's go back to South Africa about halfway through the Triassic to find out. We're in the same spot where *Lystrosaurus* was munching on *Pleuromeia* on page 8, only now the vegetation is lush and incredibly diverse.

Most of the trees and shrubs you see are gymnosperms, plants that make seeds but not flowers. They include conifers, cycads, ginkgos, and an extinct group called seed ferns (which are not ferns, despite their name). In fact, the only plants in sight that are not gymnosperms are the ferns and horsetails by the river, which are spore plants.

What you won't see are flowers. Flowering plants didn't take off until the Cretaceous period. As a result, on Valentine's Day the poor inhabitants of Pangaea had to give one another bunches of pinecones instead.

Beetles in flight

There was a huge variety of beetles, just like in our modern forests.

NEW!

Early ancestors of moths and butterflies

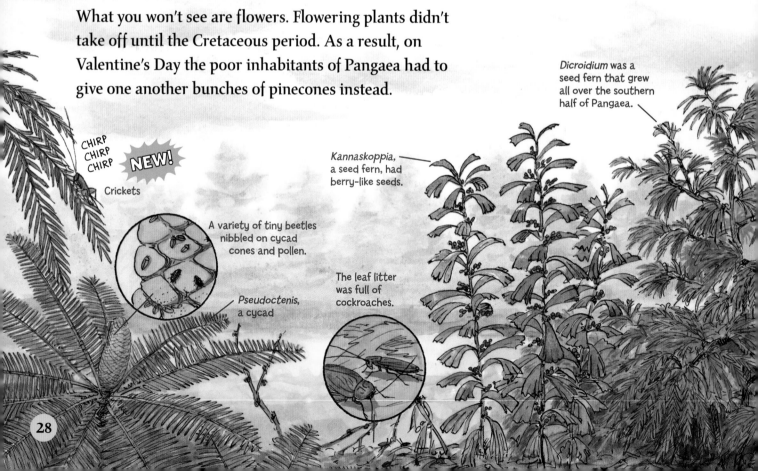

*Dicroidium* was a seed fern that grew all over the southern half of Pangaea.

CHIRP CHIRP CHIRP

NEW!

Crickets

*Kannaskoppia,* a seed fern, had berry-like seeds.

A variety of tiny beetles nibbled on cycad cones and pollen.

The leaf litter was full of cockroaches.

*Pseudoctenis,* a cycad

# A Bug Buffet

Scientists have found oodles of insect fossils among the plants. They have also found the fossilized remains of munched and tunneled leaves, chewed-out logs, nibbled cones, and other evidence that by the middle of the Triassic, insects had perfected every possible plant-eating technique.

True bugs (insects with special sucking mouthparts) were also common.

*Heidiphyllum* was a conifer with long, flat leaves instead of needles.

WE GOT MORE WAYS TO EAT A FOREST THAN ANY BUG THAT CAME BEFORE US. WE EAT POLLEN, WE DRINK SAP, WE DO THE HUNGRY INSECT RAP.

WE CAN BURROW, WE CAN SWIM, WE EAT LOGS OUT FROM WITHIN. WE EAT LEAVES AND TENDER SHOOTS, WE EAT SEEDS AND MUNCH ON ROOTS.

WE GOT MORE WAYS TO EAT A FOREST THAN ANY BUG THAT CAME BEFORE US. WE EAT POLLEN, WE DRINK SAP, WE DO THE HUNGRY INSECT RAP!

*Dicroidium* trees

Ferns

*Equisetites*, a horsetail

Drepanosaurus had a prehensile tail and a huge claw on each hand. It may have ripped open bark to get at beetle larvae. Italy. 16 in (40 cm)

Closely related, Megalancosaurus was a bit like a modern chameleon. Italy. 10 in (25 cm)

Tiny Hypuronector may have lived in the trees or in the water. U.S.A. 4.7 in (12 cm)

# A MARVELOUS MENAGERIE

ANOTHER POSSIBLE USE FOR MEGALANCOSAURUS'S TAIL HOOK...

...AND HYPURONECTOR'S WIDE TAIL.

Let's not forget the smaller creatures! Here are some of the strange beings that the Triassic cooked up to take advantage of all those bug-filled treetops above and the equally enticing bug- and fish-filled ponds below.

Some of these creatures were related to the archosaurs, and others to our modern lizards and snakes (except for the little frog next to the pond, which is, of course, an amphibian).

Odontochelys, the oldest known turtle. China. 16 in (40 cm)

Tanytrachelos was a tiny freshwater relative of super-long-necked Tanystropheus. U.S.A. 12 in (30 cm)

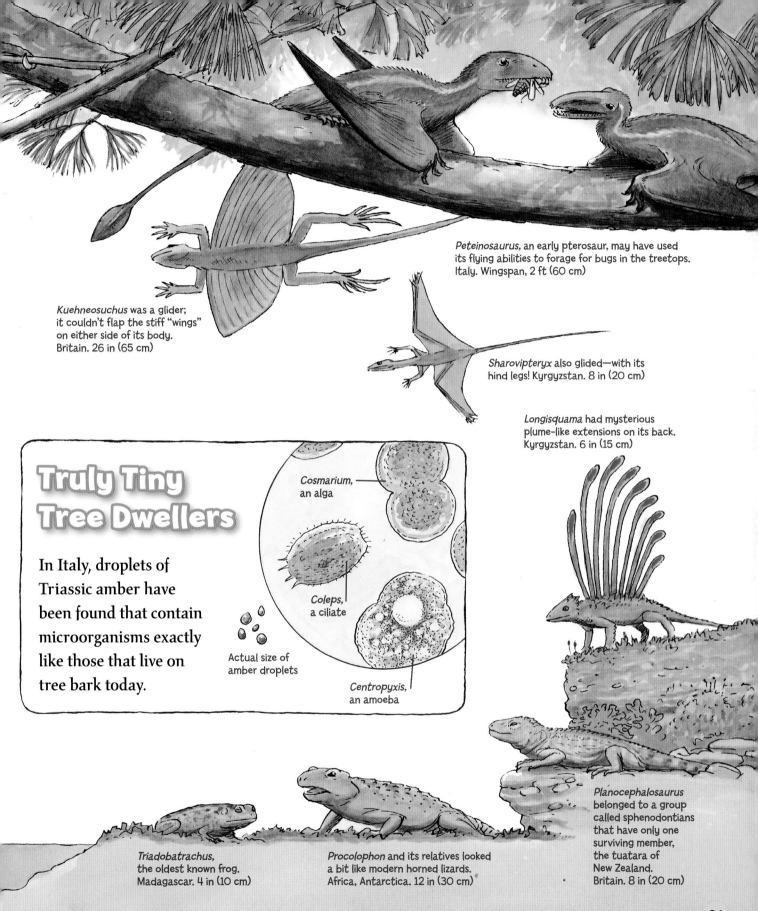

*Peteinosaurus*, an early pterosaur, may have used its flying abilities to forage for bugs in the treetops. Italy. Wingspan, 2 ft (60 cm)

*Kuehneosuchus* was a glider; it couldn't flap the stiff "wings" on either side of its body. Britain. 26 in (65 cm)

*Sharovipteryx* also glided—with its hind legs! Kyrgyzstan. 8 in (20 cm)

*Longisquama* had mysterious plume-like extensions on its back. Kyrgyzstan. 6 in (15 cm)

# Truly Tiny Tree Dwellers

In Italy, droplets of Triassic amber have been found that contain microorganisms exactly like those that live on tree bark today.

*Cosmarium*, an alga

*Coleps*, a ciliate

Actual size of amber droplets

*Centropyxis*, an amoeba

*Triadobatrachus*, the oldest known frog. Madagascar. 4 in (10 cm)

*Procolophon* and its relatives looked a bit like modern horned lizards. Africa, Antarctica. 12 in (30 cm)

*Planocephalosaurus* belonged to a group called sphenodontians that have only one surviving member, the tuatara of New Zealand. Britain. 8 in (20 cm)

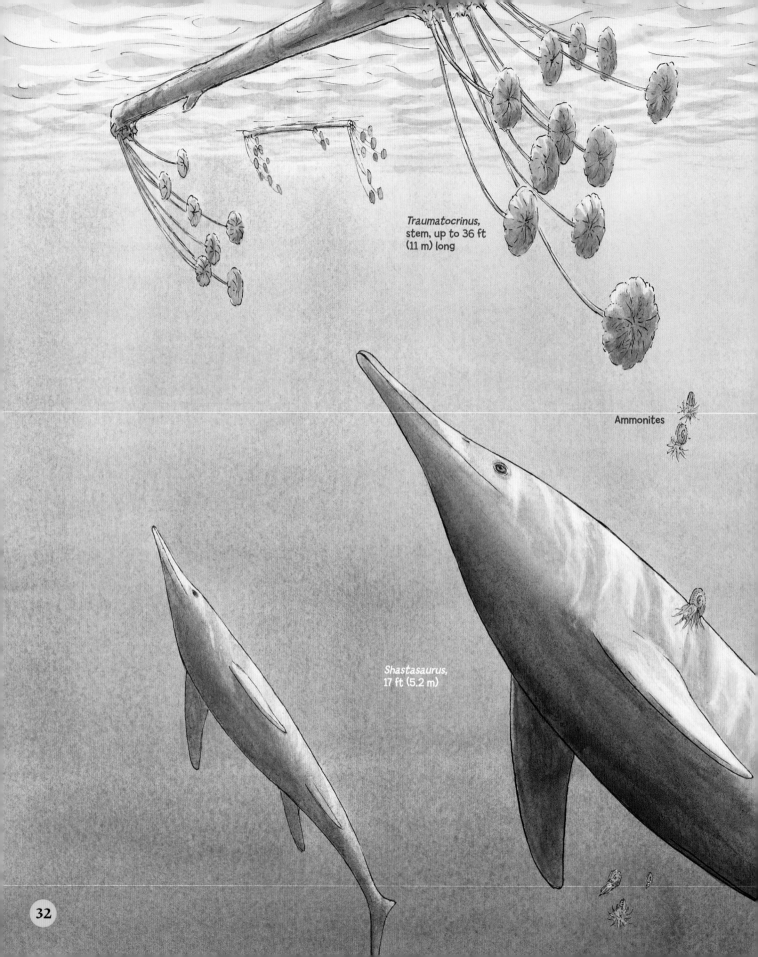

*Traumatocrinus,* stem, up to 36 ft (11 m) long

Ammonites

*Shastasaurus,* 17 ft (5.2 m)

# A Sea Change

What was happening underwater in the meantime? Let's go snorkeling in the seas of southern China in the Late Triassic to find out.

Dangling above us are crinoids, flower-shaped relatives of starfish. Normally crinoids live attached to the seafloor, but *Traumatocrinus* grew on bits of driftwood. Their feathery arms acted as nets to trap plankton as the wind pushed their driftwood rafts along.

Gliding along below are two large ichthyosaurs called *Shastasaurus*. Fear not! The *Shastasaurus* will probably ignore you; they normally eat squid and other small prey.

## First Coral Reefs

Modern reef-building corals first appeared in the Triassic. They owe their tremendous success to . . . sugar farming! Just as humans grow sugar beets or sugarcane, these corals trap and grow countless dinoflagellates (see page 20) under their "skin." The dinoflagellates are photosynthetic, meaning that they use sunlight to turn water and carbon dioxide into sugars. The corals eat these sugars to supplement what they can catch with their tentacles. The corals' waste products in turn fertilize the waters around them, which is why coral reefs are so incredibly full of life.

33

# MORPHING INTO MAMMALS

**W**e're in what is now England, peering into the rocky home of *Morganucodon*, an early mammal. Later British mammals drank tea and ate scones, but these mouse-size animals ate bugs instead, and they did so at night rather than in the afternoon. There were plenty of insects out at night, and more important, there were fewer predators. Many dinosaurs and other meat-eaters hunted by day.

Mammals didn't just appear out of nowhere. Various small therapsids became more and more mammal-like, to the point where the line between "almost-but-not-quite-mammals" and true mammals is often a little blurry. Most scientists agree that "Morgie," as *Morganucodon* is affectionately known, was indeed a true mammal. How about you? Take the test to find out.

## ARE YOU A MAMMAL?
### Standardized Test – Valid for All Pangaea

**INSTRUCTIONS:** If alive, complete whole test. If you are extinct, skip Part I since soft-tissue evidence doesn't fossilize well.

**PART I**

1. Do you stay at a constant temperature on the inside (unless you have a fever)? ............................ YES ☐ NO ☐

2. Do you have hair and/or peach fuzz anywhere on your body? ............................ YES ☐ NO ☐

3. Does your skin produce any of the following: sweat, grease, peculiar smells? ............................ YES ☐ NO ☐

4. Do you have mammary glands (breasts) or at least nipples? ............................ YES ☐ NO ☐

**PART II**

5. Is your lower jaw made up of a single bone, the dentary? (Hint: A reptile has several bones in its lower jaw.) ............................ YES ☐ NO ☐

6. Do you have teeth of different shapes for nipping, slicing, and chewing? ............................ YES ☐ NO ☐

7. Do you have three middle-ear bones, instead of just one, like reptiles? If you don't know, answer this instead: Can you hear high-pitched, squeaky sounds? ............................ YES ☐ NO ☐

**If you answered "yes" to all questions, you are a certified mammal.**

# First Dairy Products, First Fur?

Today's mammals have live babies and suckle their young. What about Morgie? We can look for clues in the duck-billed platypus, one of our most primitive living mammals. It lays eggs, and it doesn't exactly suckle its young. Instead, milk oozes onto the fur on its belly, and the babies lap it up. Triassic mammals may have laid eggs and oozed milk as well.

It is very likely that early mammals were at least somewhat warm-blooded, or endothermic, meaning that they generated heat from within. Morgie and its relatives probably had fur to help keep the warmth in, but we don't know what this fur looked like.

"ARTISTIC LICENSE"

You probably know the rest of the story. Our ancestors stayed small and dino-phobic for the rest of the Mesozoic, and it paid off: They took over the planet when the dinosaurs went extinct 150 million years later.

Lilienternus,
16 ft (5 m)

Plateosaurus,
up to 33 ft (10 m)

# A CHANGING WORLD

Proganochelys,
23 in (60 cm)

It's the rainy season in Germany, 205 million years ago. At the edge of a forest, two fast-moving *Liliensternus* are converging on a small group of *Plateosaurus*. The adult *Plateosaurus* has just heard them and has raised its head, but the theropods are unlikely to attack such a large animal: It's the younger *Plateosaurus* they're after.

*Plateosaurus* and other early long-neck dinosaurs were the biggest animals on Earth so far, and they could browse higher up in the trees than earlier plant-eaters. The theropods were also getting bigger, and dinosaurs were now the most common big animals on the planet. Even so, in many places massive crocodile-branch meat-eaters continued to be the top predators.

A PHYTOSAUR FILET, YOUR FIERCENESS?

RULING ROCKS!

**QUEEN DINO'S COURT**

The Triassic is almost over. Will it have a happy ending? Grab a sandwich, sit down at your desk, click your mouse (or your tiny early mammal, since rodents haven't evolved yet), and take a look at the online news to find out …

# The Late Triassic Times.com
### Wednesday, April 21, 205 MA

## HEARTBREAK IN PANGAEA

Rumors have surfaced that North America and Africa are beginning to drift apart. A tearful Africa declared, "We are seriously considering going our separate ways. It's sad, but after 80 million years, we're a little sick of each other."

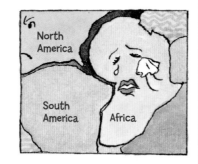

## END OF AN IDYLL

In similar news to the south, there are rumors of a possible rift between South America and its neighbors, North America and Africa.

## PANGAEA'S BROKEN HEART A GLOBAL THREAT

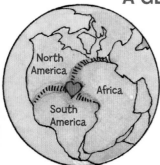

Scientists are concerned that where there once was love, there may soon be lava. The rift between the continents is opening cracks in the Earth's crust. Huge amounts of lava could spill out, along with $CO_2$ and other gases, and endanger life on the planet.

## DINOSAURS TAKE OVER,
### *says Census Bureau*

According to 205 MA census figures, dinosaurs are now the planet's most successful land animals, ahead of other archosaurs.

Census figures show very few mammals, but many may have gone uncounted due to their shy nocturnal habits and their fear of the mainly carnivorous census-takers.

*Census-taker at work*

## WEATHER

| | | |
|---|---|---|
| 99° | 102° | 103° |
| **TODAY** | **THURSDAY** | **FRIDAY** |

# EXTINCTION SANDWICH

The Triassic ended with another big extinction. Once again, volcanic activity is one of the main suspects. This time lava flowed from where Pangaea was beginning to break up into separate continents. The result was a less deadly version of the end-Permian extinction we saw on page 10.

Many marine creatures died. On land, the plants didn't do too badly. Mammals survived (obviously, or you wouldn't be reading this), and so did the dinosaurs and pterosaurs. The crocodile relatives weren't so lucky: Only the crocodiles themselves survived. The moment the curtain lifted on the next period, the Jurassic, the dinosaurs looked around, saw they had the place to themselves, and immediately grew bigger and meaner, becoming the true rulers of Pangaea. But that's a whole other story!

THE END

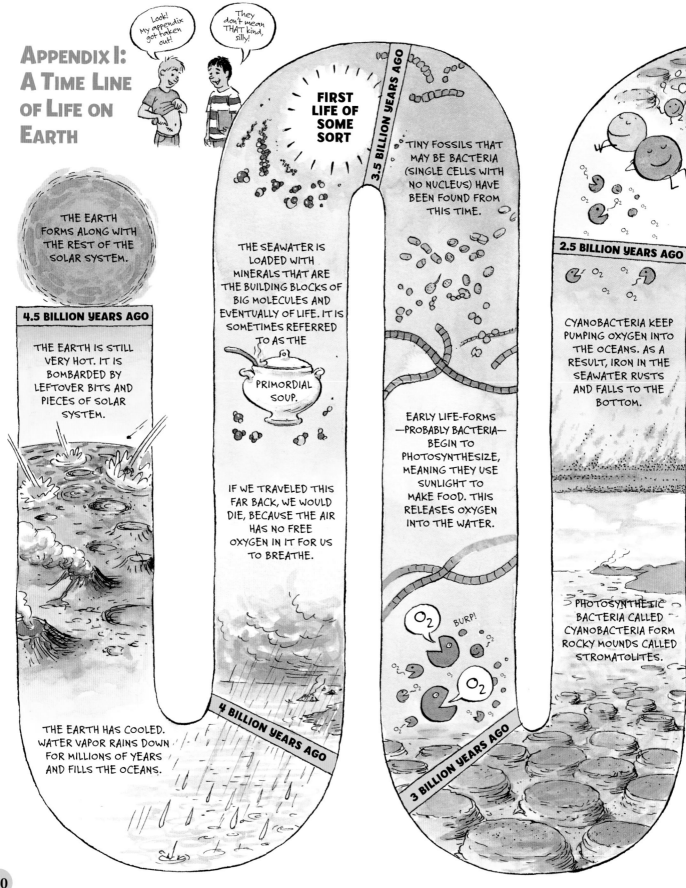

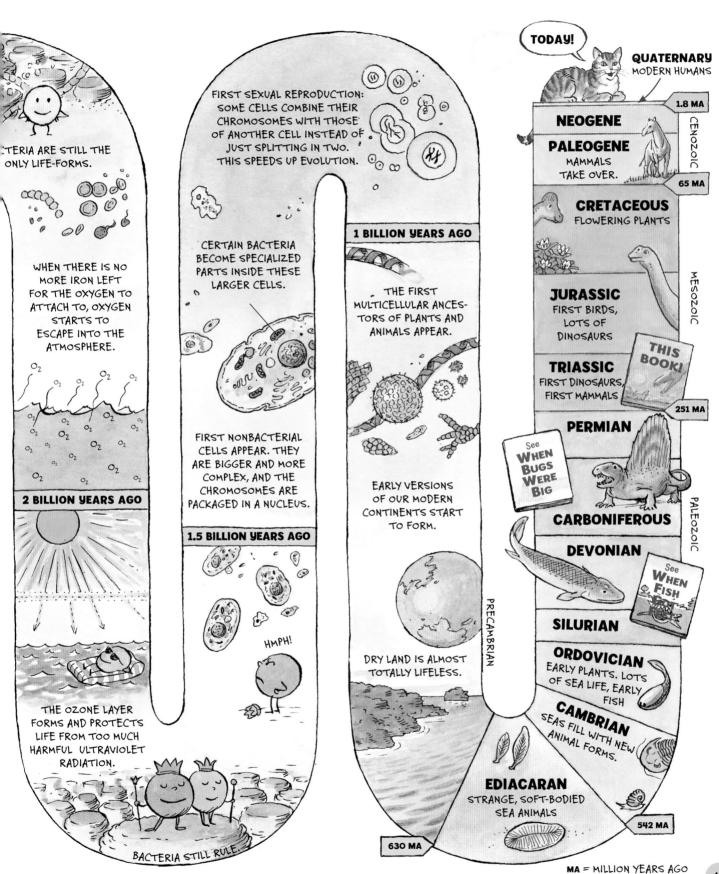

BACTERIA ARE STILL THE ONLY LIFE-FORMS.

WHEN THERE IS NO MORE IRON LEFT FOR THE OXYGEN TO ATTACH TO, OXYGEN STARTS TO ESCAPE INTO THE ATMOSPHERE.

2 BILLION YEARS AGO

THE OZONE LAYER FORMS AND PROTECTS LIFE FROM TOO MUCH HARMFUL ULTRAVIOLET RADIATION.

BACTERIA STILL RULE.

FIRST SEXUAL REPRODUCTION: SOME CELLS COMBINE THEIR CHROMOSOMES WITH THOSE OF ANOTHER CELL INSTEAD OF JUST SPLITTING IN TWO. THIS SPEEDS UP EVOLUTION.

CERTAIN BACTERIA BECOME SPECIALIZED PARTS INSIDE THESE LARGER CELLS.

FIRST NONBACTERIAL CELLS APPEAR. THEY ARE BIGGER AND MORE COMPLEX, AND THE CHROMOSOMES ARE PACKAGED IN A NUCLEUS.

1.5 BILLION YEARS AGO

HMPH!

1 BILLION YEARS AGO

THE FIRST MULTICELLULAR ANCESTORS OF PLANTS AND ANIMALS APPEAR.

EARLY VERSIONS OF OUR MODERN CONTINENTS START TO FORM.

DRY LAND IS ALMOST TOTALLY LIFELESS.

PRECAMBRIAN

630 MA

TODAY!

QUATERNARY
MODERN HUMANS

1.8 MA

NEOGENE

PALEOGENE
MAMMALS TAKE OVER.

65 MA

CENOZOIC

CRETACEOUS
FLOWERING PLANTS

JURASSIC
FIRST BIRDS, LOTS OF DINOSAURS

THIS BOOK!

TRIASSIC
FIRST DINOSAURS, FIRST MAMMALS

251 MA

MESOZOIC

PERMIAN

See WHEN BUGS WERE BIG

CARBONIFEROUS

DEVONIAN

See WHEN FISH

PALEOZOIC

SILURIAN

ORDOVICIAN
EARLY PLANTS. LOTS OF SEA LIFE, EARLY FISH

CAMBRIAN
SEAS FILL WITH NEW ANIMAL FORMS.

EDIACARAN
STRANGE, SOFT-BODIED SEA ANIMALS

542 MA

MA = MILLION YEARS AGO

# Appendix II: Our Tetrapod Family Tree

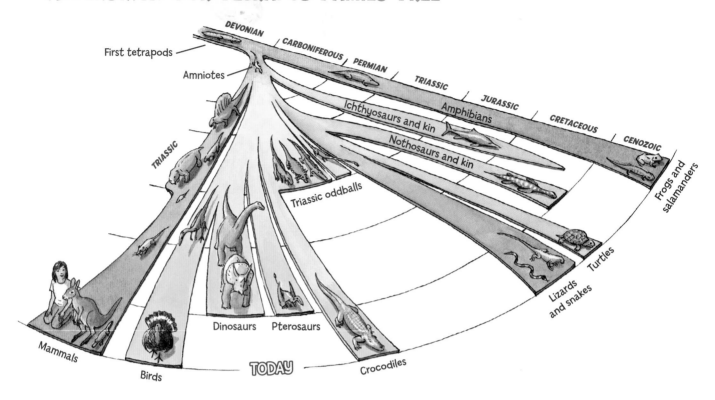

First tetrapods
Amniotes
DEVONIAN
CARBONIFEROUS
PERMIAN
TRIASSIC
JURASSIC
CRETACEOUS
CENOZOIC
Ichthyosaurs and kin
Amphibians
Nothosaurs and kin
TRIASSIC
Triassic oddballs
Frogs and salamanders
Turtles
Lizards and snakes
Mammals
Birds
Dinosaurs
Pterosaurs
Crocodiles
TODAY

## Some Notes From Hannah

**LATIN NAMES**  The scientific names I've used in this book refer to the genus to which a living being belongs. A genus is a group of closely related species. Dogs, wolves, and coyotes, for instance, all belong to the same genus, *Canis*, but to different species: *Canis familiaris*, *Canis lupus*, and *Canis latrans*, respectively. If you go to a museum and see a *Lystrosaurus* that looks different from the one I show on page 8, it might be a different species. The one on page 8 is *Lystrosaurus murrayi*.

**THINGS CHANGE**  Paleontologists are constantly discovering new fossils, and each new fossil adds a piece to the puzzle of what life was like in the distant past. It is possible that in a few years some of the things I describe in this book may be better understood. Feathered dinosaurs are a good example. I show *Herrerasaurus* and *Liliensternus* without feathers, but if some amazingly preserved fossils show up that prove even these very early dinosaurs had feathers, I'll be ripping out my hair in frustration and wishing I could go back and add feathers to the theropods in this book.

**WHERE TO FIND OUT MORE**  Natural history museums are wonderful, but if you're not lucky enough to live near one, you can at least go to their Web sites to see what's in them. Web sites that belong to a museum or a university are great because you can trust them to give accurate information. A good example is the in-depth information about evolution at http://evolution.berkeley

.edu/. For maps of the prehistoric world, go to www.scotese.com, click on "Earth History," and then choose a time period. There are also some science-heavy but really good blogs about the Triassic and about paleontology in general, such as Archosaur Musings (www.archosaurmusings.wordpress.com) and the Hairy Museum of Natural History (www.hmnh.org). Wikipedia has tons of good information, mixed in with the occasional blooper; I'd say it's about 80 percent reliable. It can also be fun to use a search engine such as Google to search for "Triassic period" and see what you get. Just remember that anyone can set up a Web site, including people who don't know what they're talking about, so be a little bit skeptical as you browse the Web.

The most complete book about the Triassic is *Dawn of the Dinosaurs, Life in the Triassic*, by Nicholas Fraser. It's for grownups and is highly scientific, but it has beautiful illustrations by Doug Henderson, my favorite paleo-artist, that make you feel as if you are right there in the Triassic.

If, my dear reader, you are sitting and reading this in the U.S.A., you are in a magnificent position to pester your parents to take you to amazing Triassic fossil sites such as the Petrified Forest in Arizona. If your parents refuse to drive that far, find out whether your home state has rocks from the Triassic by going to the Paleontology Portal, http://www.paleoportal.org, and clicking on "Exploring Time and Space" for a map of the U.S.A. with information on the geology and fossil sites of every state.

# HOW TO PRONOUNCE SOME OF THE SCIENTIFIC TERMS IN THIS BOOK

**Aethophyllum** (ee-tho-FILL-um)

**Bjuvia** (BYOO-vee-ah)

**Cambrian** (KAM-bree-an)

**Canis** (KAY-nus)

**Carboniferous** (kar-bon-IF-er-us)

**Cenozoic** (sen-oh-ZO-ik)

**Coccolithophore** (coc-co-LITH-o-fore)

**Coelophysis** (see-luh-FY-sis)

**Cretaceous** (kre-TAY-shus)

**Crinoid** (KRY-noid)

**Cymbospondylus** (sim-bus-PON-di-lus)

**Desmatosuchus** (des-ma-to-SOO-kus)

**Devonian** (de-VONE-ee-an)

**Dicroidium** (dy-cro-ID-ee-um)

**Dinoflagellate** (DY-no-FLAJ-el-ate)

**Drepanosaurus**
(dreh-PAN-o-SAWR-us)

**Ediacaran** (EE-dee-AK-ar-un)

**Effigia** (eh-fih-JEE-uh)

**Eocyclotosaurus**
(EE-oh-cy-CLO-tuh-SAWR-us)

**Eudimorphodon**
(yoo-dy-MOR-foh-don)

**Exaeretodon** (ex-a-REHT-uh-don)

**Fungi** (FUN-guy or FUNJ-eye)

**Gondwana** (gon-DWON-ah)

**Herrerasaurus** (He-REH-ruh-SAWR-us)

**Hesperosuchus** (HES-pe-roh-SOO-kus)

**Hyperodapedon**
(HY-per-o-DAP-eh-don)

**Jurassic** (jur-ASS-ik)

**Kuehneosuchus** (KOO-nee-o-SOO-kus)

**Lepocyclotes** (lep-o-seye-CLO-tees)

**Liliensternus** (LIH-lee-en-STER-nus)

**Longisquama** (lon-jih-SKWAM-uh)

**Lotosaurus** (LOH-toh-SAWR-us)

**Lystrosaurus** (lis-tru-SAWR-us)

**Massetognathus**
(MASS-eh-tog-NAYTH-us)

**Mesozoic** (meh-zuh-ZO-ik)

**Morganucodon**
(MOR-gu-NOO-kuh-don)

**Neusticosaurus** (noos-tik-o-SAWR-us)

**Nothosaurus** (noth-uh-SAWR-us)

**Odontochelys** (o-don-tuh-KEE-leez)

**Ordovician** (or-do-VISH-ee-an)

**Paleogene** (PAY-lee-oh-jeen)

**Paleozoic** (pay-lee-oh-ZO-ik)

**Panphagia** (pan-FAY-jee-uh)

**Panthalassa** (pan-thal-AH-suh)

**Pelourdea** (pel-OOR-dee-ah)

**Permian** (PURR-mee-an)

**Phytosaur** (FYE-tuh-sawr)

**Pisanosaurus** (pih-ZAN-uh-SAWR-us)

**Plateosaurus** (plat-e-o-SAWR-us)

**Postosuchus** (po-sto-SOO-kus)

**Procolophon** (pro-KAH-luh-fon)

**Proganochelys** (pro-gan-o-KEE-leez)

**Protrachyceras** (pro-trak-ih-SER-us)

**Pseudopalatus** (SOO-doe-puh-LAY-tus)

**Ptilozamites** (til-o-zum-EYE-tees)

**Quaternary** (kwa-TER-ner-ee)

**Sharovipteryx** (shar-o-VIP-ter-ix)

**Silurian** (si-LURE-ee-an)

**Sinokannemeyeria**
(SY-no-KAN-uh-my-EH-ree-a)

**Tanystropheus** (tan-iss-TRO-fee-us)

**Tethys** (TETH-iss)

**Thalattosaur** (ta-LAT-uh-sawr)

**Thrinaxodon** (thrin-AX-uh-don)

**Ticinosuchus** (ti-SEEN-o-SOOK-us)

**Traumatocrinus** (traw-mat-o-CRY-nus)

**Triadobatrachus**
(try-AD-o-ba-TRAY-kus)

**Triassic** (try-ASS-ik)

**Triops cancriformis**
(TRY-ops can-kri-FOR-mis)

**Voltzia** (VOL-tsee-uh)

# GLOSSARY OF WORDS NOT DEFINED IN THE TEXT

**Ammonite:** An extinct cephalopod (see below) with a coiled shell.

**Amniote:** A four-legged animal whose young are protected in a bag of liquid called amnion until they hatch or are born. This allows the amniote to develop on dry land, unlike an amphibian, which has to lay its eggs in water.

**Amphibian:** A four-legged animal that spends at least part of its life in water, where it lays its eggs.

**Bacteria:** Microscopic single-cell life-forms with a distinctive kind of cell wall and no nucleus.

**Cephalopod:** A group of marine animals like squid and octopus that have tentacles sprouting from their head region (cephalopod means "head-foot").

**$CO_2$:** Carbon dioxide, a gas that is present in small amounts in the air. Plants need it in order to breathe. It is one of the greenhouse gases, so called because they trap heat from the sun and make the planet warmer.

**Cycad:** A kind of gymnosperm, or non-flowering seed plant, that looks like a small palm tree. Cycads still exist in warm climates today.

**Fungi (singular: fungus):** The group that includes mushrooms, yeast, and molds. Fungi do not photosynthesize and cannot make their own food from scratch as plants can. Instead, they recycle nutrients created by plants and other life-forms.

**Ginkgo:** A common Mesozoic tree with a characteristic fan-shaped leaf. Only one species, *Ginkgo biloba*, has survived to this day.

**Ozone layer:** A layer of ozone ($O_3$, a form of oxygen with a strong odor) surrounding the Earth 10 to 12 miles above its surface.

**Plankton:** Tiny animals and other life-forms that drift in the water and are a source of food for many larger animals.

**Prehensile tail:** A strong tail that can wrap around a branch so that its owner doesn't fall. Opossums, chameleons, and seahorses have prehensile tails.

**Scavenger:** An animal that eats the remains of dead animals that it finds.

**Tetrapod:** An animal with four legs. Reptiles, amphibians, and mammals are tetrapods.

**Ultraviolet radiation:** Also known as UV light, it is a form of light that we can't see but that causes sunburn.

# INDEX

# AUTHOR'S SOURCES FOR TEXT AND IMAGES

## Books

Carroll, Robert. *The Rise of Amphibians: 265 Million Years of Evolution.* Baltimore, MD: The Johns Hopkins University Press, 2009.

Clarkson, E. N. K. *Invertebrate Paleontology and Evolution.* Oxford: Blackwell Science, 1998.

Cowen, Richard. *History of Life.* Malden, MA: Blackwell Publishing, 2005.

Cox, Barry, et al. *Mackmillan Illustrated Encyclopedia of Dinosaurs and Prehistoric Creatures.* New York: Simon and Schuster, 1999.

Fraser, Nicholas. *Dawn of the Dinosaurs: Life in the Triassic.* Bloomington: Indiana University Press, 2006.

Grimaldi, David A. and Michael S. Engel. *Evolution of the Insects.* New York: Cambridge University Press, 2005.

Kielan-Jaworowska, Zofia, Richard L. Cifelli, and Zhe-Xi Luo. *Mammals from the Age of Dinosaurs: Origins, Evolution, and Structure.* New York: Columbia University Press, 2004.

Long, John A. *The Rise of Fishes.* Baltimore, MD: The Johns Hopkins University Press, 1995.

Looy, C. V. *The Permian-Triassic Biotic Crisis: Collapse and Recovery of Terrestrial Ecosystems.* Utrecht, Netherlands: Utrecht University, 2000.

Maisey, John G. *Discovering Fossil Fishes.* Boulder, CO: Westview Press, 2000.

Steyer, Sébastien, and Alain Bénéteau. *La Terre Avant Les Dinosaures.* Paris: Belin, 2009.

Sues, Hans-Dieter, and Nicholas Fraser. *Triassic Life on Land: The Great Transition.* New York: Columbia University Press, 2010.

Taylor, Thomas N., Edith Taylor, and Michael Krings. *Paleobotany: The Biology and Evolution of Fossil Plants.* Burlington, MA: Academic Press, 2009.

Wellnhofer, Dr. Peter, and John Sibbick. *Historia Ilustrada de los Pterosaurios.* Madrid, Spain: Susaeta Ediciones, 2003.

Wood, Rachel. *Reef Evolution.* New York: Oxford University Press, 1999.

## Articles

Anderson, John M., Heidi M. Anderson, and Arthur R. I. Cruikshank. "Late Triassic ecosystems of the Molteno/ Lower Elliot Biome of Southern Africa" *Palaeontology* 41, part 3 (1889): 387—421.

Botha, Jennifer, and Roger M. H. Smith. "Lystrosaurus species composition across the Permo—Triassic boundary in the Karoo Basin of South Africa." *Lethaia* 40 (2007): 125—137.

Brusatte, Stephen L., Michael J. Benton, Julia B. Desojo, and Max C. Langer. "The higher-level phylogeny of Archosauria (Tetrapoda: Diapsida)." *Journal of Systematic Palaeontology* 8 (2010): 1, 3—47.

Falkowski, Paul G., et al. 2004. " The evolution of modern eukaryotic phytoplankton." *Science* 305: 354—360.

Fuchs, Günter, Léa Grauvogel-Stamm, and Detlef Mader. 1991. "Une remarquable foret à Pleuromeia et Anomopteris in situ du Buntsandstein moyen." *Palaeontographica* Abt. B 222 Lfg. 4—6, 89—120.

Grauvogel-Stamm, Léa, and Sidney R. Ash. 2005. "Recovery of the Triassic land flora from the end-Permian life crisis." *Palevol* 4: 525—540.

Grauvogel-Stamm, Léa, and Bernard Lugardon. 2001. "The Triassic Lycopsids Pleuromeia and Annalepis: relationships, evolution, and origin." *American Fern Journal* 91(3): 115.

Kerp, Hans, Michael Krings, and Christian Pott. 2008. "The Carnian (Late Triassic) flora from Lunz in Lower Austria: paleoecological considerations." *Palaeoworld* 17: 172—182.

Kidder, D. L., and T. R. Worsley. "Phanerozoic Large Igneous Provinces (LIPs), HEATT (Haline Euxinic Acidic Thermal Transgression) episodes, and mass extinctions." *Palaeogeography, Palaeoclimatology, Palaeoecology* 295, no. 1—2 (2010): 162—191.

Kustatscher, E., and J. H. A. Van Konijnenburg-van Cittert. "The Ladinian Flora (Middle Triassic) of the Dolomites: palaeoen- vironmental reconstructions and palaeoclimatic consider- ations." *Geo. Alp* 2 (2005): 31—51.

Li, Chun, et al. "An ancestral turtle from the Late Triassic of Southwestern China." *Nature* 456 (2008): 497—501.

McElwain, Jennifer C., and Surangi W. Punyasena. "Mass extinc- tion events and the plant fossil record." *TRENDS in Ecology and Evolution* 22, no. 10 (2007).

Morel, E. M., A. E. Artabe, and L. A. Spalletti. "Triassic floras of Argentina: biostratigraphy, floristic events and comparison with other areas of Gondwana and Laurasia." *Alcheringa* 27 (2003): 231—243.

Müller J. "Early loss and multiple return of the lower temporal arcade in diapsid reptiles." *Naturwissenschaften* 90, no. 10 (2003): 473—6.

Preto, Nereo, Evelyn Kustatscher, and Paul B. Wignall. "Triassic Climate—state of the art and perspectives." *Palaeogeography, Palaeoclimatology, Palaeoecology* 290 (2010): 1—10.

Reichow, Marc K., et al. "The timing and extent of the eruption of the Siberian Traps large igneous province: Implications for the end-Permian environmental crisis." *Earth and Planetary Science Letters* 277, no. 1—2 (2009): 9—20.

Roghi, Guido, Eugenio Ragazzi, and Piero Gianollo. 2006. "Triassic amber of the Southern Alps (Italy)." *Palaios* 21: 143—154.

Taylor, Edith L., and Thomas N. Taylor. "Fossil tree rings and Paleoclimate from the Triassic of Antarctica." *New Mexico Museum of Natural History & Science Bulletin* No. 3, (1993).

X. Wang, G. H. et al. 2008. "The Late Triassic black shales of the Guanling area, Guizhou province, south-west China: a unique marine reptile and pelagic crinoid fossil lagerstätte." *Palaeontology.* 51, no. 1 (1993): 27—61.

Whiteside, Jessica H., et al. "Compound-specific carbon isotopes from Earth's largest flood basalt eruptions directly linked to the end-Triassic mass extinction 2010." *PNAS,* vol. 107, no. 15 (2010): 6721—6725.

## Web Sites

A great many Web sites were helpful in researching this book. A tiny sample follows:

Palaeos, www.palaeos.com

The highly informative UC Berkeley site, www.ucmp.berkeley.edu

The Paleomap project, www.scotese.com and Ron Blakey's site, http://jan.ucc.nau.edu/~rcb7/paleogeographic.html were the main sources for Paleomaps.

The International Commission on Stratigraphy, www.stratigra phy.org/cheu.pdf is the source of the dates in the time lines.